CROCK·POT
◆ THE ORIGINAL SLOW COOKER ◆

5 INGREDIENTS
or Less

Publications International, Ltd.

pilcookbooks.com

Pictured on the front cover: Easy Cheesy Barbecue Chicken *(page 68).*
Pictured on the back cover (clockwise from top): Asian Beef with Broccoli *(page 80),* Cheesy Corn and Peppers *(page 104)* and Chorizo Chili *(page 44).*

pilcookbooks.com

TABLE OF CONTENTS

INTRODUCTION

Slow Cooking Hints and Tips

Slow Cooker Sizes

Smaller slow cookers, such as 1- to 3½-quart models, are the perfect size for singles, a couple, empty-nesters and for serving dips.

While medium-size slow cookers (those holding somewhere between 3 and 5 quarts) will easily cook enough food to feed a small family, they're also convenient for holiday side dishes and appetizers.

Large slow cookers are great for big family dinners, holiday entertaining, and potluck suppers. A 6- to 7-quart model is ideal if you like to make meals in advance and have dinner tonight and store leftovers for another day.

Types of Slow Cookers

Current models of **CROCK-POT®** slow cookers come equipped with many different features and benefits, from auto-cook programs, to stovetop-safe stoneware, to timed programming.

Visit www.crockpot.com to find the slow cooker that best suits your needs and lifestyle.

Cooking, Stirring, and Food Safety

CROCK-POT® slow cookers are safe to leave unattended. The outer heating base may get hot as it cooks, but it should not pose a fire hazard. The heating element in the heating base functions at a low wattage and is safe for your countertops.

Your slow cooker should be filled at least one-half to three-quarters full for most recipes unless otherwise instructed. Lean meats, such as chicken or pork tenderloin, will cook faster than meats with more connective tissue and fat, such as beef chuck or pork shoulder. Bone-in meats will take longer than boneless cuts. Typical slow cooker dishes take

7 to 8 hours to reach the simmer point on LOW and 3 to 4 hours on HIGH. Once the vegetables and meat begin to simmer and braise, their flavors will fully blend and the meat will become fall-off-the bone tender.

According to the United States Department of Agriculture, all bacteria are killed at a temperature of 165°F. It's important to follow the recommended cooking times and to avoid opening the lid often, especially early in the cooking process when heat is building up inside the unit. If you need to open the lid to check on your food or are adding additional ingredients, remember to allow additional cooking time, if necessary, to ensure food is thoroughly cooked and tender.

Large slow cookers, the 6- to 7-quart sizes, may benefit from a quick stir halfway through the cook time to help distribute heat and promote even cooking. It is usually unnecessary to stir at all since even ½ cup of liquid will help to distribute heat, and the crockery is the perfect medium for holding food at an even temperature throughout the cooking process.

Oven-Safe

All **CROCK-POT®** slow cooker removable crockery inserts may (without their lids) be used in ovens at up to 400°F safely. Also, all **CROCK-POT®** crockery inserts are microwavable without their lids. If you own another brand slow cooker, please refer to your owner's manual for advice on oven and microwave safety.

Frozen Food

Frozen or partially frozen food can be cooked in a slow cooker; however, it will require a longer cooking time than the same recipe made with fresh food. Using an instant-read thermometer is recommended to ensure meat is completely cooked.

Pasta and Rice

If you're converting a recipe that calls for uncooked pasta, cook the pasta according to the package directions just until tender before adding it to the slow cooker. If you are converting a recipe that calls for cooked rice, stir in the raw rice with other ingredients; add ¼ cup of extra liquid per ¼ cup of raw rice.

Beans

Beans must be softened completely before they're combined with sugar and/or acidic foods. Sugar and acid have a hardening effect on beans and

will prevent softening. Fully cooked canned beans may be used as a substitute for dried beans.

Vegetables

Root vegetables often cook more slowly than meat. Cut vegetables into small pieces so that they cook at the same rate as the meat, large or small, lean or marbled. Place them near the sides or on the bottom of the stoneware so that they will cook more quickly.

Herbs

Fresh herbs add flavor and color when they're added at the end of the cooking time, but for dishes with shorter cook times, hearty fresh herbs such as rosemary and thyme hold up well. If added at the beginning, the flavor of many fresh herbs lessen over long cook times. Ground and/or dried herbs and spices work well in slow cooking because they retain their flavor, and may be added at beginning.

The flavor power of all herbs and spices can vary greatly depending on their particular strength and shelf life. Use chili powders and garlic powder sparingly because they often intensify over long cook times. Always taste the finished dish and adjust the seasonings, including salt and pepper, before serving.

Liquids

It's not necessary to use more than ½ to 1 cup of liquid in most instances since the juices in meats and vegetables are retained in slow cooking more so than in conventional cooking. Excess liquid can be reduced and concentrated after slow cooking either on the stovetop or by removing meat and vegetables from stoneware, stirring in cornstarch or tapioca, and setting the slow cooker to HIGH. Cook on HIGH for approximately 15 minutes or until the juices are thickened.

Milk

Milk, cream, and sour cream break down during extended cooking. When possible, add them during the last 15 to 30 minutes of cooking, until just heated through. Condensed soups may be substituted for milk and can cook for extended times.

Fish

Fish is delicate and it should be stirred in gently during the last 15 to 30 minutes of cooking time. Cook just until cooked through, and serve immediately.

5 Ingredients or Less

A well-stocked pantry is a shortcut to preparing meals efficiently. This chapter takes full advantage of the kinds of everyday ingredients most cooks commonly have on hand by featuring recipes which can be created using no more than 5 ingredients in addition to these pantry items and any items listed as "optional" in the ingredients list:

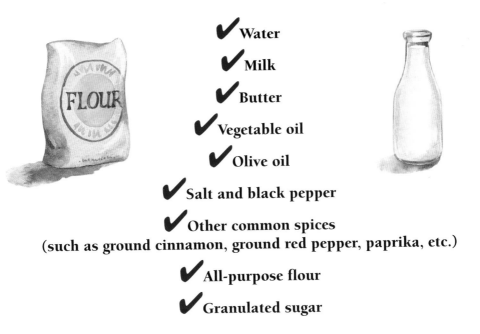

✔ **Water**

✔ **Milk**

✔ **Butter**

✔ **Vegetable oil**

✔ **Olive oil**

✔ **Salt and black pepper**

✔ **Other common spices**
(such as ground cinnamon, ground red pepper, paprika, etc.)

✔ **All-purpose flour**

✔ **Granulated sugar**

These recipes are perfect for busy days when you don't have time to make another stop at the grocery store. Check the following pages for everything from hearty stews to simple sides, from roast beef to chocolate pudding cake and everything in between.

EASY BEEF ENTRÉES

Easy Beef Stew

2 pounds beef stew meat, cut into 1-inch cubes

1 can (4 ounces) mushrooms

1 envelope (1 ounce) dry onion soup mix

1 can (10¾ ounces) condensed cream of mushroom soup, undiluted

⅓ cup red or white wine

Hot cooked noodles (optional)

Combine beef, mushrooms, soup mix, soup and wine in **CROCK-POT®** slow cooker. Cover; cook on LOW 8 to 12 hours. Serve over noodles, if desired.

Makes 4 to 6 servings

Tip: *Browning the beef before cooking it in the **CROCK-POT®** slow cooker isn't necessary but helps to enhance the flavor and appearance of the stew. If you have the time, use nonstick cooking spray and brown the meat in a large skillet before placing it in the **CROCK-POT®** slow cooker; follow the recipe as written.*

EASY BEEF ENTRÉES

Bacon and Onion Brisket

6 slices bacon, cut crosswise into ½-inch strips

1 flat-cut boneless brisket (about 2½ pounds)

Salt and black pepper

3 medium onions, sliced

2 cans (10¾ ounces each) condensed beef consommé, undiluted

1. Cook bacon strips in large skillet over medium-high heat about 3 minutes. Do not overcook. Transfer bacon with slotted spoon to **CROCK-POT®** slow cooker.

2. Season brisket with salt and pepper. Return skillet to medium-high heat and sear brisket in hot bacon fat on all sides, turning as it browns. Transfer to **CROCK-POT®** slow cooker.

3. Lower skillet heat to medium. Add sliced onions to skillet. Cook and stir 3 to 5 minutes or until softened. Add to **CROCK-POT®** slow cooker. Pour in consommé. Cover; cook on HIGH 6 to 8 hours or until meat is tender.

4. Transfer brisket to cutting board and let rest 10 minutes. Slice brisket against the grain into thin slices, and arrange on platter. Add salt and pepper, if desired. Spoon bacon, onions and cooking liquid over brisket to serve.

Makes 6 servings

EASY BEEF ENTRÉES

French Onion Soup

¼ cup (½ stick) butter

3 pounds yellow onions, sliced

1 tablespoon sugar

2 to 3 tablespoons dry white wine or water (optional)

2 quarts (8 cups) beef broth

8 to 16 slices French bread (optional)

½ cup (2 ounces) shredded Gruyère or Swiss cheese (optional)

1. Melt butter in large skillet over medium to low heat. Add onions; cover and cook just until onions are tender and transparent, but not browned, about 10 minutes.

2. Remove cover. Sprinkle sugar over onions. Cook and stir 8 to 10 minutes or until onions are caramelized. Add onions and any browned bits to **CROCK-POT®** slow cooker. If desired, add wine to pan. Bring to a boil, scraping up any browned bits. Add to **CROCK-POT®** slow cooker. Stir in broth. Cover; cook on LOW 8 hours or on HIGH 6 hours.

3. Preheat broiler. To serve, ladle soup into individual soup bowls. If desired, top each with 1 or 2 bread slices and about 1 tablespoon cheese. Place under broiler until cheese is melted and bubbly.

Makes 8 servings

Variation: *Substitute 1 cup dry white wine for 1 cup of the beef broth.*

EASY BEEF ENTRÉES

Tavern Burger

2 pounds 95% lean ground beef

½ cup ketchup

¼ cup packed brown sugar

¼ cup prepared yellow mustard

Hamburger buns

1. Cook beef in medium skillet over medium-high heat until no longer pink, stirring to break up meat. Drain fat. Transfer beef to **CROCK-POT®** slow cooker.

2. Add ketchup, sugar and mustard to **CROCK-POT®** slow cooker; mix well. Cover; cook on LOW 4 to 6 hours. Serve on buns.

Makes 8 servings

Tip: *Serve a scoopful on a hamburger bun. This is also known to some people as "BBQ's" or "loose-meat sandwiches." For added flavor, add a can of pork and beans when adding the other ingredients.*

Veggie Soup with Beef

2 cans (15 ounces each) mixed vegetables

1 pound beef stew meat

1 can (8 ounces) tomato sauce

2 cloves garlic, minced

Water

Place all ingredients in **CROCK-POT®** slow cooker. Add enough water to fill **CROCK-POT®** slow cooker to within ½ inch of top. Cover; cook on LOW 8 to 10 hours.

Makes 4 servings

Tavern Burger

EASY BEEF ENTRÉES

Swiss Steak Stew

2 to 3 boneless beef top
  sirloin steaks (about
  4 pounds)

2 cans (about 14 ounces
  each) diced tomatoes,
  undrained

2 medium green bell
  peppers, cut into ½-inch
  strips

2 medium onions, chopped

1 tablespoon seasoned salt

1 teaspoon black pepper

Cut each steak into 3 to 4 pieces; place in **CROCK-POT®** slow cooker. Add tomatoes with juice, bell peppers and onions. Season with salt and pepper. Cover; cook on LOW 8 hours or until meat is tender.

Makes 10 servings

Dad's Dill Beef Roast

1 beef chuck roast
  (3 to 4 pounds)

1 large jar whole dill pickles,
  undrained

Place beef in **CROCK-POT®** slow cooker. Pour pickles with juice over top of beef. Cover; cook on LOW 8 to 10 hours. Remove beef to platter and shred with two forks.

Makes 6 to 8 servings

Serving Suggestion: *Pile this beef onto toasted rolls or buns or, for an easy dinner variation, serve it with mashed potatoes.*

Swiss Steak Stew

EASY BEEF ENTRÉES

Royal Roundsteak

1 to 2 pounds roundsteak or
   stew meat cubes

1 to 2 tablespoons oil

1 envelope (1 ounce)
   dry onion soup mix

2 cans cream of mushroom
   soup

   Hot cooked rice or cooked
   egg noodles

1. Trim roundsteak and cut into cubes. (Partially freeze meat for easier cutting.)

2. Heat oil in large skillet over medium-high heat. Brown meat on all sides.

3. Combine dry soup mix and canned soup in mixing bowl. Pour into **CROCK-POT®** slow cooker. Add browned meat. Cover; cook on HIGH 6 to 7 hours.

4. To serve, spoon over prepared rice or egg noodles.

Makes 6 servings

Country-Style Steak

4 to 6 beef cube steaks

   All-purpose flour

1 tablespoon vegetable oil

1 envelope (1 ounce)
   dry onion soup mix

1 envelope (1 ounce)
   brown gravy mix

   Water

1. Dust steaks with flour. Heat oil in large skillet over medium-low heat. Brown steaks on both sides. Drain fat. Transfer steaks to **CROCK-POT®** slow cooker.

2. Add soup and gravy mixes and enough water to cover meat. Cover; cook on LOW 6 to 8 hours.

Makes 4 to 6 servings

Serving Suggestion: *Serve with mashed potatoes.*

Royal Roundsteak

EASY BEEF ENTRÉES

Easy Chili

1 teaspoon vegetable oil

1 pound 95% lean ground beef

1 medium onion, chopped

2 cans (10¾ ounces each) condensed tomato soup, undiluted

1 cup water

Salt and black pepper

Chili powder

1. Heat oil in large skillet over medium-high heat. Add beef and onion. Cook and stir until beef is well browned. Drain excess fat.

2. Place meat mixture, soup and water in **CROCK-POT®** slow cooker. Add salt, pepper and chili powder to taste. Cover; cook on LOW 6 hours.

Makes 4 servings

Tip: *This dish can cook up to 8 hours. Garnish with shredded cheese and serve with crackers or thick slices of Italian bread.*

Autumn Delight

1 tablespoon olive oil

4 to 6 beef cubed steaks

2 cans (10¾ ounces each) condensed cream of mushroom soup, undiluted

1 cup water

1 package (1 ounce) dry onion soup mix or mushroom soup mix

1. Heat oil in large skillet over medium heat until hot. Lightly brown steaks on both sides. Transfer to **CROCK-POT®** slow cooker.

2. Combine soup, water and dry soup mix in large bowl; mix well. Pour over steaks. Cover; cook on LOW 4 to 6 hours.

Makes 4 to 6 servings

Easy Chili

So Simple Supper!

1 **beef chuck shoulder roast (3 to 4 pounds)**

1 **envelope (1 ounce) au jus gravy mix**

1 **envelope (1 ounce) onion soup mix**

1 **envelope (1 ounce) mushroom gravy mix**

3 **cups water**

Assorted vegetables (potatoes, carrots, onions and celery)

1. Place roast in **CROCK-POT®** slow cooker. Combine soup and gravy mixes and water in large bowl. Pour mixture over roast. Cover; cook on LOW 4 hours.

2. Add vegetables. Cover; cook 4 hours more or until meat and vegetables are tender.

Makes 8 servings

EASY BEEF ENTRÉES

Best-Ever Roast

1 beef chuck shoulder roast
(3 to 5 pounds)

1 can (10¾ ounces)
condensed cream of
mushroom soup, undiluted

1 envelope (1 ounce)
dry onion soup mix

4 to 5 medium potatoes,
quartered

4 cups baby carrots

1. Place roast in **CROCK-POT®** slow cooker. (If necessary, cut roast in half to fit into **CROCK-POT®** slow cooker.) Combine mushroom soup and onion soup mix in medium bowl. Pour over roast. Cover; cook on LOW 4 hours.

2. Add potatoes and carrots. Cover; cook on LOW 2 hours.

Makes 6 to 8 servings

Smothered Steak

4 to 6 beef cubed beef
steaks (about 1½ to
2 pounds)

All-purpose flour

1 can (10¾ ounces)
condensed cream of
mushroom soup, undiluted

1 package (1 ounce) dry
onion soup mix

Hot cooked rice (optional)

1. Dust steaks lightly with flour. Place in **CROCK-POT®** slow cooker. Combine mushroom soup and onion soup mix in medium bowl. Pour over steak.

2. Cover; cook on LOW 6 to 8 hours. Serve over rice, if desired.

Makes 4 servings

24

Best-Ever Roast

EASY BEEF ENTRÉES

Easy Beef Sandwiches

1 large onion, sliced

1 boneless beef bottom round roast (about 3 to 5 pounds)

1 cup water

1 envelope (1 ounce) au jus gravy mix

French bread, sliced lengthwise

Provolone cheese (optional)

1. Place onion slices in bottom of **CROCK-POT®** slow cooker; top with roast. Combine water and gravy mix in small bowl; pour over roast. Cover and cook on LOW 7 to 9 hours.

2. Shred meat using two forks. Serve on French bread, topped with cheese, if desired. Serve cooking liquid on the side for dipping.

Makes 6 to 8 servings

EASY BEEF ENTRÉES

Peppered Beef Tips

1 pound beef round tip roast or round steak, cut into 1- to 1½-inch pieces

2 cloves garlic, minced

Black pepper

1 can (10¾ ounces) condensed French onion soup, undiluted

1 can (10¾ ounces) condensed cream of mushroom soup, undiluted

Hot cooked noodles or rice

1. Place beef in **CROCK-POT®** slow cooker. Season with garlic and pepper. Pour soups over beef.

2. Cover; cook on LOW 8 to 10 hours. Serve over noodles.

Makes 2 to 3 servings

Serving Suggestion: *Serve these beef tips over cooked noodles or rice.*

PORK DISHES

Boneless Pork Roast With Garlic

1 **boneless pork rib roast (2 to 2½ pounds), rinsed and patted dry**

Salt and black pepper, to taste

3 **tablespoons olive oil, divided**

4 **garlic cloves, minced**

4 **tablespoons chopped fresh rosemary**

½ **lemon, cut into ⅛- to ¼-inch slices**

¼ **cup white wine**

½ **cup chicken stock**

1. Unroll the pork roast and season with salt and black pepper. Combine 2 tablespoons oil, garlic and rosemary in small bowl. Rub over pork.

2. Roll and tie pork snugly with twine. Tuck lemon slices under twine and into ends of roast.

3. Heat remaining 1 tablespoon oil in skillet over medium heat until hot. Sear pork on all sides until just browned. Transfer to **CROCK-POT®** slow cooker.

4. Return skillet to heat. Add white wine and stock, stirring with wooden spoon to loosen any caramelized bits. Pour over pork. Cover; cook on LOW 8 to 9 hours or on HIGH 3½ to 4 hours.

5. Transfer roast to cutting board. Allow to rest for 10 minutes before removing twine and slicing. Adjust seasonings, if desired. To serve, pour pan juices over sliced pork.

Makes 4 to 6 servings

PORK DISHES

Steamed Pork Buns

½ **container (18 ounces) refrigerated shredded cooked pork in barbecue sauce***

1 **tablespoon Asian garlic chili sauce**

1 **container (about 16 ounces) large refrigerated biscuits (8 biscuits)**

Dipping Sauce (recipe follows)

Sliced green onions (optional)

Look for pork in plain, not smoky, barbecue sauce. Substitute with chicken in barbecue sauce, if desired.

1. Combine pork and chili sauce in medium bowl. Split biscuits in half. Roll or stretch each biscuit half into 4-inch circle. Spoon 1 tablespoon pork onto center of each bottom. Cover with biscuit top, gather edges around filling and press to seal.

2. Generously butter 2-quart baking dish that fits inside **CROCK-POT®** slow cooker. Arrange filled biscuits in single layer, overlapping slightly if necessary. Cover dish with buttered foil, buttered side down.

3. Place small rack in **CROCK-POT®** slow cooker. Add 1 inch hot water (water should not come to top of rack). Place baking dish on rack. Cover; cook on HIGH 2 hours.

4. Meanwhile, prepare Dipping Sauce. Garnish pork buns with green onions, if desired. Serve with Dipping Sauce.

Makes 8 servings

Dipping Sauce: *Stir together 2 tablespoons rice vinegar, 2 tablespoons reduced-sodium soy sauce, 4 teaspoons sugar and 1 teaspoon toasted sesame oil in a small bowl until sugar dissolves.*

PORK DISHES

Rough-Cut Smoky Red Pork Roast

1 **pork shoulder roast (about 4 pounds)**

1 **can (14½ ounces) stewed tomatoes, drained**

1 **can (6 ounces) tomato paste with basil, oregano and garlic**

1 **cup chopped red bell pepper**

2 **to 3 canned chipotle peppers in adobo sauce, finely chopped and mashed with fork***

1 **teaspoon salt**

1½ **to 2 tablespoons sugar**

For less heat, remove seeds from chipotle peppers before mashing

1. Coat **CROCK-POT®** slow cooker with nonstick cooking spray. Place pork, fat side up, in bottom. Combine remaining ingredients, except sugar, in small bowl. Pour over pork.

2. Cover; cook on HIGH 5 hours. Scrape tomato mixture into cooking liquid. Transfer pork to cutting board; let stand 15 minutes.

3. Stir sugar into cooking liquid. Cook, uncovered, on HIGH 15 minutes longer. To serve, remove fat from pork and slice. Pour sauce over pork slices.

Makes 8 servings

PORK DISHES

Scalloped Potatoes & Ham

6 large russet potatoes,
   sliced into ¼-inch rounds

1 ham steak (about 1½
   pounds), cut into cubes

1 can (10¾ ounces)
   condensed cream of
   mushroom soup, undiluted

1 soup can water

1 cup (4 ounces) shredded
   Cheddar cheese

   Grill seasoning to taste

1. Spray inside of **CROCK-POT®** slow cooker with nonstick cooking spray. Layer potatoes and ham in **CROCK-POT®** slow cooker.

2. In large mixing bowl, combine soup, water, cheese and seasoning; pour over potatoes and ham.

3. Cover; cook on HIGH about 3½ hours or until potatoes are fork-tender. Turn **CROCK-POT®** slow cooker to LOW and continue cooking about 1 hour or until done.

Makes 5 to 6 servings

PORK DISHES

Slow Cooked Pork & Sauerkraut

2 jars (32 ounces each) sauerkraut, drained and rinsed

1 envelope (1 ounce) dry onion soup mix

3 tablespoons brown mustard

2½ cups water

3 pounds boneless pork loin roast

Combine sauerkraut, soup mix, mustard and water in large mixing bowl. Mix well, then add with pork to **CROCK-POT®** slow cooker. Cover; cook on LOW 8 hours.

Makes 6 servings

Savory Slow Cooker Pork Roast

1 (3- to 4-pound) boneless pork blade or sirloin roast

Salt and black pepper

2 tablespoons vegetable oil

1 medium onion, sliced in ¼-inch-thick rings

2 to 3 cloves of garlic, chopped

1 can (15 ounces) chicken broth

1. Season pork with salt and pepper. Heat oil in large skillet over medium heat; brown roast on all sides.

2. Place onion slices on bottom of **CROCK-POT®** slow cooker; sprinkle with garlic. Place roast on onions; pour chicken broth over roast.

3. Cover; cook on LOW 10 hours or on HIGH 6 to 7 hours.

Makes 8 servings

Slow Cooked Pork & Sauerkraut

PORK DISHES

Shredded Pork Wraps

1 cup salsa, divided

2 tablespoons cornstarch

1 boneless pork loin roast (2 pounds)

6 (8-inch) flour tortillas

3 cups broccoli slaw mix

½ cup (2 ounces) shredded Cheddar cheese (optional)

1. Combine ¼ cup salsa and cornstarch in small bowl; stir until smooth. Pour mixture into **CROCK-POT®** slow cooker. Top with pork roast. Pour remaining ¾ cup salsa over roast. Cover; cook on LOW 6 to 8 hours.

2. Transfer roast to cutting board. Trim and discard fat from pork. Pull pork into coarse shreds using 2 forks.

3. Divide shredded meat evenly among tortillas. Spoon about 2 tablespoons salsa mixture on top of meat in each tortilla. Top evenly with broccoli slaw and cheese, if desired. Fold bottom edge of tortilla over filling; fold in sides. Roll up completely to enclose filling. Serve remaining salsa mixture as dipping sauce.

Makes 6 servings

PORK DISHES

Old-Fashioned Split Pea Soup

- **4 quarts chicken broth**
- **2 pounds dried split peas**
- **1 cup chopped ham**
- **½ cup chopped onion**
- **½ cup chopped celery**
- **2 teaspoons salt**
- **2 teaspoons black pepper**

1. Place all ingredients in **CROCK-POT®** slow cooker. Stir well to combine. Cover; cook on LOW 8 to 10 hours or on HIGH 4 to 6 hours or until peas are soft.

2. Mix with hand mixer or hand blender on low speed until smooth.

Makes 8 servings

Buck County Ribs

- **4 to 6 boneless pork country-style ribs**
- **1 teaspoon salt**
- **1 jar (about 28 ounces) sauerkraut, drained**
- **1 medium apple, diced**
- **1 tablespoon sugar**
- **1 cup chicken broth or 1 cup water plus 1 teaspoon chicken bouillon granules**
- **Mashed potatoes (optional)**

1. Place ribs in **CROCK-POT®** slow cooker. Sprinkle with salt.

2. Spoon sauerkraut over ribs. Top with apple. Sprinkle sugar over apple. Add chicken broth. Cover; cook on LOW 8 to 9 hours. Serve with mashed potatoes, if desired.

Makes 4 to 6 servings

Old-Fashioned Split Pea Soup

PORK DISHES

Chorizo Chili

1 **pound 90% lean ground beef**

8 **ounces raw chorizo sausage, removed from casings**

1 **can (16 ounces) chili beans in chili sauce**

2 **cans (14½ ounces each) zesty chili-style diced tomatoes, undrained**

1. Place beef and chorizo in **CROCK-POT®** slow cooker. Stir to break up well.

2. Stir in beans and tomatoes. Cover; cook on LOW 7 hours. Skim off and discard excess fat before serving.

Makes 6 servings

Serving Suggestion: *Top with sour cream or shredded cheese.*

Easy Pork Chop Dinner

1 **large onion, thinly sliced**

3 **to 4 medium baking potatoes, sliced**

6 **pork chops**

1 **can (10¾ ounces) condensed reduced-fat cream of celery soup, undiluted**

½ **cup water or milk**

1. Place onion and potatoes in **CROCK-POT®** slow cooker. Top with pork chops.

2. Combine soup and water in small bowl; pour over chops. Cover; cook on LOW 6 to 8 hours.

Makes 6 servings

Tip: *Serve with salad or vegetables for a delicious dinner.*

44

Chorizo Chili

PORK DISHES

Easy Homemade Barbecue Sandwiches

Water

1 boneless pork shoulder roast (3 to 4 pounds)

Salt and black pepper to taste

1 bottle (16 ounces) barbecue sauce

8 hamburger buns or sandwich rolls, toasted

1. Cover bottom of **CROCK-POT®** slow cooker with 1 inch water. Place roast in **CROCK-POT®** slow cooker; season with salt and pepper, if desired. Cover; cook on LOW 8 to 10 hours.

2. Remove roast from **CROCK-POT®** slow cooker; let stand 15 minutes. Discard liquid remaining in **CROCK-POT®** slow cooker. Shred cooked roast using 2 forks.

3. Return meat to **CROCK-POT®** slow cooker. Add barbecue sauce; mix well. Cover and cook on HIGH 30 minutes. Serve barbecue mixture on buns.

Makes 8 to 10 servings

Tip: *Depending on the size of your roast, you may not need to use an entire bottle of barbecue sauce. This recipe is equally tasty when made with other cuts of pork roast.*

PORK DISHES

Polska Kielbasa with Beer 'n Onions

⅓ cup honey mustard

⅓ cup packed dark brown sugar

18 ounces brown ale or beer

2 kielbasa sausages (16 ounces each), cut into 4-inch pieces

2 onions, quartered

Combine honey mustard and brown sugar in **CROCK-POT®** slow cooker. Whisk in ale. Add sausage pieces. Top with onions. Cover; cook on LOW 4 to 5 hours, stirring occasionally.

Makes 6 to 8 servings

Simply Delicious Pork

1½ pounds boneless pork loin, cut into 6 pieces *or* 6 boneless pork loin chops

4 medium Golden Delicious apples, sliced

3 tablespoons packed brown sugar

1 teaspoon ground cinnamon

½ teaspoon salt

1. Place pork in **CROCK-POT®** slow cooker; cover with apples.

2. Combine brown sugar, cinnamon and salt in small bowl; sprinkle over apples. Cover; cook on LOW 6 to 8 hours.

Makes 6 servings

Polska Kielbasa with Beer 'n Onions

PORK DISHES

Simple Shredded Pork Tacos

2 pounds boneless pork
  roast

1 cup salsa

1 can (4 ounces) chopped
  green chiles

½ teaspoon garlic salt

½ teaspoon black pepper

  Flour or corn tortillas

  Optional toppings:
  salsa, sour cream, diced
  tomatoes, shredded
  cheese, shredded lettuce

1. Place roast, salsa, chiles, garlic salt and pepper in **CROCK-POT®** slow cooker. Cover; cook on LOW 8 hours, or until meat is tender.

2. Remove pork from **CROCK-POT®** slow cooker; shred with 2 forks. Serve on flour tortillas with sauce. Top as desired.

Makes 6 servings

CHICKEN & TURKEY

Slow Cooker Chicken and Dressing

4 boneless, skinless chicken breasts

Salt and black pepper

4 slices Swiss cheese

1 can (14½ ounces) chicken broth

2 cans (10¾ ounces each) condensed cream of chicken, celery or mushroom soup, undiluted

3 cups packaged stuffing mix

½ cup (1 stick) butter, melted

1. Place chicken in **CROCK-POT®** slow cooker. Season with salt and pepper.

2. Top each breast with cheese slice. Add broth and soup. Sprinkle stuffing mix over top; pour melted butter over all. Cover; cook on LOW 6 to 8 hours or on HIGH 3 to 4 hours.

Makes 4 servings

CHICKEN & TURKEY

Slow Cooker Chicken Dinner

4 boneless, skinless chicken breasts

1 can (10¾ ounces) condensed cream of chicken soup, undiluted

⅓ cup milk

1 package (6 ounces) stuffing mix

1⅔ cups water

Place chicken in **CROCK-POT®** slow cooker. Combine soup and milk in small bowl; mix well. Pour soup mixture over chicken. Combine stuffing mix and water. Spoon stuffing over chicken. Cover; cook on LOW 6 to 8 hours.

Makes 4 servings

CHICKEN & TURKEY

Spicy Turkey with Citrus Au Jus

1 bone-in turkey breast, thawed, rinsed and patted dry (about 4 pounds)

4 tablespoons (½ stick) butter, at room temperature

Grated peel of 1 medium lemon

1 teaspoon chili powder

¼ to ½ teaspoon black pepper

⅛ to ¼ teaspoon red pepper flakes

1 tablespoon lemon juice

Salt and black pepper

1. Coat **CROCK-POT®** slow cooker with nonstick cooking spray. Add turkey breast.

2. Mix butter, lemon peel, chili powder, black pepper and pepper flakes in small bowl until well blended. Spread mixture over top and sides of turkey. Cover; cook on LOW 4 to 5 hours or on HIGH 2½ to 3 hours or until meat thermometer reaches 165°F and juices run clear. Do not overcook.

3. Transfer turkey to cutting board. Let stand 10 minutes before slicing. Turn **CROCK-POT®** slow cooker to LOW.

4. Stir lemon juice into cooking liquid. Pour mixture through fine-mesh sieve; discard solids in sieve. Let mixture stand 5 minutes. Skim and discard excess fat. Add salt and pepper, if desired. Return au jus mixture to **CROCK-POT®** slow cooker. Cover to keep warm. Serve au jus with turkey.

Makes 6 to 8 servings

CHICKEN & TURKEY

Creamy Chicken

3 boneless, skinless chicken breasts *or* 6 boneless, skinless chicken thighs

2 cans (10¾ ounces each) condensed cream of chicken soup, undiluted

1 can (14½ ounces) chicken broth

1 can (4 ounces) sliced mushrooms, drained

½ medium onion, diced

Salt and black pepper

Hot cooked pasta (optional)

Place all ingredients except salt and pepper in **CROCK-POT®** slow cooker. Cover and cook on LOW 6 to 8 hours. Season to taste with salt and pepper. Serve over pasta, if desired.

Makes 3 servings

Tip: *If desired, you may add 8 ounces of cubed pasteurized processed cheese spread before serving.*

CHICKEN & TURKEY

Chicken & Biscuits

4 boneless, skinless chicken breasts

1 can (10¾) ounces) condensed cream of chicken soup

1 package (10 ounces) frozen peas and carrots

1 package (7½ ounces) refrigerated biscuits

1. Cut chicken breasts into bite-size pieces. Place in **CROCK-POT®** slow cooker. Pour soup over chicken. Cover; cook on LOW 4 hours or until chicken is tender and no longer pink in center.

2. Stir in frozen vegetables. Cover and cook 30 minutes longer until vegetables are heated through.

3. Bake biscuits according to package directions. Spoon chicken and vegetable mixture over biscuits and serve.

Makes 4 servings

Spicy Shredded Chicken

6 boneless, skinless chicken breasts (about 1½ pounds)

1 jar (16 ounces) salsa

Place chicken in **CROCK-POT®** slow cooker. Pour salsa over chicken. Cover; cook on LOW 6 to 8 hours or until chicken is tender and no longer pink in center. Shred chicken with 2 forks before serving.

Makes 6 servings

Serving Suggestion: *Serve on warm flour tortillas with taco fixings.*

Chicken & Biscuits

CHICKEN & TURKEY

Herbed Turkey Breast with Orange Sauce

1 large onion, chopped

3 cloves garlic, minced

1 teaspoon dried rosemary

½ teaspoon black pepper

1 boneless, skinless turkey breast (3 pounds)

1½ cups orange juice

1. Place onion in **CROCK-POT®** slow cooker. Combine garlic, rosemary and pepper in small bowl; set aside. Cut slices about three-fourths of the way through turkey at 2-inch intervals. Rub garlic mixture between slices.

2. Place turkey, cut side up, in **CROCK-POT®** slow cooker. Pour orange juice over turkey. Cover; cook on LOW 7 to 8 hours.

3. Serve sauce from **CROCK-POT®** slow cooker with sliced turkey.

Makes 6 servings

CHICKEN & TURKEY

Slow Cooker Turkey Breast

½ **to 1 teaspoon garlic powder, or to taste**

½ **to 1 teaspoon paprika, or to taste**

1 **turkey breast (4 to 6 pounds)**

1 **tablespoon dried parsley flakes, or to taste**

1. Blend garlic powder and paprika. Rub into turkey skin. Place turkey in **CROCK-POT®** slow cooker. Sprinkle on parsley. Cover; cook on low 6 to 8 hours or on high 2½ to 3 hours or until internal temperature reaches 165°F when meat thermometer is inserted into thickest part of breast, not touching bone.

2. Transfer turkey to cutting board; cover with foil and let stand 10 to 15 minutes before carving. (Internal temperature will rise 5° to 10°F during stand time.)

Makes 4 to 6 servings

CHICKEN & TURKEY

BBQ Turkey Legs

6 turkey drumsticks

2 teaspoons salt

2 teaspoons black pepper

1 bottle (16 ounces)
   barbecue sauce

Season drumsticks with salt and pepper. Place in **CROCK-POT®** slow cooker. Add barbecue sauce, and turn drumsticks to coat evenly. Cover; cook on LOW 7 to 8 hours or on HIGH 3 to 4 hours. Enjoy hot or cold.

Makes 6 servings

Cheesy Slow Cooker Chicken

6 boneless, skinless chicken
   breasts (about 1½ pounds)

   Salt and black pepper

   Garlic powder

2 cans (10¾ ounces each)
   condensed cream of
   chicken soup, undiluted

1 can (10¾ ounces)
   condensed Cheddar
   cheese soup, undiluted

   Chopped fresh parsley
   (optional)

1. Place 3 chicken breasts in **CROCK-POT®** slow cooker. Sprinkle with salt, pepper and garlic powder. Repeat with remaining 3 breasts and seasonings.

2. Combine soups in medium bowl; pour over chicken. Cover; cook on LOW 6 to 8 hours or until chicken is tender. Garnish with parsley, if desired.

Makes 6 servings

Serving Suggestion: *The sauce is wonderful over pasta, rice or mashed potatoes.*

BBQ Turkey Legs

Easy Cheesy Barbecue Chicken

6 boneless skinless chicken breasts (about 1½ pounds)

1 bottle (26 ounces) barbecue sauce

6 slices bacon

6 slices Swiss cheese

1. Place chicken in **CROCK-POT®** slow cooker. Cover with barbecue sauce. Cover; cook on LOW 8 to 9 hours. (If sauce becomes too thick during cooking, add a little water.)

2. Before serving, cut bacon slices in half. Cook bacon in microwave or on stove top, keeping bacon flat. Place 2 pieces cooked bacon on each chicken breast in **CROCK-POT®** slow cooker. Top with cheese. Cover; cook on HIGH until cheese melts.

Makes 6 servings

Tip: *To make cleanup easier, coat the inside of the **CROCK-POT®** slow cooker with nonstick cooking spray before adding the ingredients. To remove any sticky barbecue sauce residue, soak the stoneware in hot sudsy water, then scrub it with a plastic or nylon scrubber; don't use steel wool.*

CHICKEN & TURKEY

Heidi's Chicken Supreme

1 can (10¾ ounces)
  condensed cream of
  chicken soup, undiluted

1 envelope (1 ounce)
  dry onion soup mix

6 boneless, skinless chicken
  breasts (about 1½ pounds)

½ cup imitation bacon bits or
  ½ pound bacon, crisp-
  cooked and crumbled

1 container (16 ounces)
  reduced-fat sour cream

1. Spray **CROCK-POT®** slow cooker with nonstick cooking spray. Combine soup and soup mix in medium bowl; mix well. Layer chicken breasts and soup mixture in **CROCK-POT®** slow cooker. Sprinkle with bacon.

2. Cover; cook on HIGH 4 hours or on LOW 8 hours.

3. During last hour of cooking, stir in sour cream.

Makes 6 servings

Tip: *Condensed cream of mushroom soup or condensed cream of celery soup can be substituted for cream of chicken soup.*

CHICKEN & TURKEY

Chicken Sausage Pilaf

1 pound chicken or turkey
   sausage, casings removed

1 cup uncooked rice and
   vermicelli pasta mix

4 cups chicken broth

2 stalks celery, diced

¼ cup slivered almonds

   Salt and black pepper

1. Brown sausage in large skillet over medium-high heat, stirring to break up meat. Drain fat. Add rice and pasta mix to skillet. Cook and stir 1 minute.

2. Place mixture in **CROCK-POT®** slow cooker. Add broth, celery, almonds, salt and pepper to **CROCK-POT®** slow cooker; mix well.

3. Cover; cook on LOW 7 to 10 hours or on HIGH 3 to 4 hours or until rice is tender.

Makes 4 servings

ETHNIC RECIPES

Carne Rellenos

1 can (4 ounces) whole
  green chiles, drained

4 ounces cream cheese,
  softened

1 flank steak (about
  2 pounds)

1½ cups salsa verde

1. Slit whole chiles open on one side with sharp knife; stuff with cream cheese.

2. Open steak flat on sheet of waxed paper; score steak and turn over. Lay stuffed chiles across unscored side of steak. Roll up and tie with kitchen string.

3. Place steak in **CROCK-POT®** slow cooker; pour in salsa. Cover; cook on LOW 6 to 8 hours or on HIGH 3 to 4 hours or until done.

4. Remove steak and cut into 6 pieces. Serve with sauce.

Makes 6 servings

ETHNIC RECIPES

Mango Ginger Pork Roast

1 pork shoulder roast
(about 4 pounds)

½ to 1 teaspoon ground
ginger, or to taste

Salt and black pepper

2 cups mango salsa

2 tablespoons honey

¼ cup apricot preserves

Hot cooked rice (optional)

1. Season roast with ginger, salt and pepper to taste. Transfer to **CROCK-POT®** slow cooker.

2. Combine salsa, honey and preserves. Pour over roast. Cover; cook on LOW 6 to 8 hours. Turn **CROCK-POT®** slow cooker to HIGH and cook 3 to 4 hours longer or until roast is tender. Serve over rice, if desired.

Makes 4 to 6 servings

Easy Beef Stroganoff

3 cans (10¾ ounces each)
condensed cream of
mushroom soup, undiluted

1 cup sour cream

½ cup water

1 envelope (1 ounce)
dry onion soup mix

2 pounds beef stew meat

Combine soup, sour cream, water and onion soup mix in **CROCK-POT®**slow cooker. Add beef; stir until well coated. Cover; cook on LOW 6 hours or on HIGH 3 hours.

Makes 4 to 6 servings

Serving Suggestion: *Serve this beef over hot cooked wild rice or noodles along with a salad and grilled bread.*

Tip: *You can reduce the calories and fat in this dish by using 98% fat-free soup and fat-free sour cream.*

Mango Ginger Pork Roast

ETHNIC RECIPES

Sandy's Mexican Chicken

2 to 4 chicken breasts

1 medium onion, sliced

1 can (10¾ ounces) condensed cream of chicken soup, undiluted

1 can (10 ounces) Mexican-style diced tomatoes with green chiles, undrained

1 package (8 ounces) pasteurized process cheese spread, cubed

1. Place chicken, onion, soup, and tomatoes with chiles in **CROCK-POT®** slow cooker. Cover; cook on LOW 6 to 8 hours or on HIGH 4 hours.

2. Break up chicken into pieces. Add cheese spread; cook on HIGH until melted.

Makes 2 to 4 servings

Serving Suggestion: *Serve over hot cooked spaghetti.*

Asian Beef with Broccoli

1½ pounds boneless chuck steak, about 1½ inches thick, sliced thin*

1 can (10½ ounces) beef consommé

½ cup oyster sauce

2 tablespoons cornstarch

1 bag (16 ounces) fresh broccoli florets

Hot cooked rice (optional)

Sesame seeds (optional)

To make slicing steak easier, place in freezer for 30 minutes before slicing.

1. Place steak in **CROCK-POT®** slow cooker. Pour consommé and oyster sauce over meat. Cover; cook on HIGH 3 hours.

2. Combine cornstarch and 2 tablespoons cooking liquid in a cup. Add to **CROCK-POT®** slow cooker. Stir well to combine. Cover; cook 15 minutes longer or until thickened.

3. Poke holes in broccoli bag with fork. Microwave on HIGH (100%) 3 minutes. Empty bag into **CROCK-POT®** slow cooker. Gently toss beef and broccoli together. Serve over cooked rice and garnish with sesame seeds, if desired.

Makes 4 to 6 servings

ETHNIC RECIPES

Super-Easy Beef Burritos

1 boneless beef chuck roast
(2 to 3 pounds)

1 can (28 ounces) enchilada
sauce

Water (optional)

4 (8-inch) flour tortillas

1. Place roast in **CROCK-POT®** slow cooker; cover with enchilada sauce. Add 2 to 3 tablespoons water, if desired.

2. Cover; cook on LOW 6 to 8 hours or until beef begins to fall apart. Shred beef; serve in tortillas.

Makes 4 servings

Serving Suggestion: *Excellent garnishes include shredded cheese, sour cream, salsa, lettuce and tomatoes.*

Knockwurst and Cabbage

Olive oil

8 to 10 knockwurst
sausages

1 head red cabbage, cut into
¼-inch slices

½ cup thinly sliced white
onion

2 teaspoon caraway seeds

1 teaspoon salt

4 cups chicken broth

1. Heat oil in skillet over medium heat until hot. Brown knockwursts on all sides, turning as they brown. Transfer to **CROCK-POT®** slow cooker.

2. Add cabbage and onion. Sprinkle with caraway seeds and salt. Add broth. Cover; cook on LOW 4 hours or on HIGH about 2 hours, or until knockwursts are cooked through and cabbage and onions are soft.

Makes 8 servings

Super-Easy Beef Burritos

ETHNIC RECIPES

Corned Beef and Cabbage

1 head cabbage (1½ pounds), cut into 6 wedges

1 bag (4 ounces) baby carrots

1 corned beef (3 pounds) with seasoning packet*

1 quart (4 cups) water

⅓ cup prepared mustard

⅓ cup honey

*If seasoning packet is not perforated, poke several small holes with tip of paring knife.

1. Place cabbage in **CROCK-POT®** slow cooker; top with carrots. Place seasoning packet on top of vegetables. Place corned beef, fat side up, over seasoning packet and vegetables. Add water. Cover; cook on LOW 10 hours.

2. Combine mustard and honey in small bowl.

3. Discard seasoning packet. Slice beef and serve with vegetables and mustard sauce.

Makes 6 servings

ETHNIC RECIPES

Chili Verde

1 tablespoon vegetable oil

1 to 2 pounds boneless pork chops

Sliced carrots (enough to cover bottom of CROCK-POT® slow cooker)

1 jar (24 ounces) mild salsa verde

Chopped onion (optional)

1. Heat oil in large skillet over medium-low heat. Brown pork on both sides. Drain excess fat.

2. Place carrot slices in bottom of **CROCK-POT®** slow cooker. Place pork on top of carrots. Pour salsa over chops. Add onion, if desired. Cover; cook on HIGH 6 to 8 hours.

Makes 4 to 8 servings

Serving Suggestion: *If desired, shred the pork and serve it with tortillas.*

Orange Chicken

1 can (12 ounces) orange soda

½ cup soy sauce

4 boneless, skinless chicken breasts (about 1 pound)

Hot cooked rice

Pour soda and soy sauce in **CROCK-POT®** slow cooker. Add chicken and turn to coat. Cover; cook on LOW 5 to 6 hours. Serve over rice.

Makes 4 servings

Chili Verde

ETHNIC RECIPES

Best Asian-Style Ribs

2 full racks baby back pork
   ribs, split into 3 sections
   each

6 ounces hoisin sauce

2 tablespoons minced fresh
   ginger

½ cup maraschino cherries

½ cup rice wine vinegar

   Water to cover

4 green onions, chopped
   (optional)

Combine ribs, hoisin sauce, ginger, cherries, vinegar and water in the **CROCK-POT®** slow cooker. Cover; cook on LOW 6 to 7 hours or on HIGH 3 to 3½ hours or until pork is done. Sprinkle with green onions before serving, if desired.

Makes 6 to 8 servings

Hot & Sour Chicken

4 to 6 boneless, skinless chicken breasts (1 to 1½ pounds)

1 cup chicken or vegetable broth

1 envelope (1 ounce) dry hot-and-sour soup mix

Place chicken in **CROCK-POT®** slow cooker. Add broth and soup mix. Cover; cook on LOW 5 to 6 hours. Garnish as desired.

Makes 4 to 6 servings

Serving Suggestion: *For a nutritious and colorful variation from traditional steamed white rice, serve this dish over a bed of snow peas and sugar snap peas tossed with diced red bell pepper.*

Mile-High Enchilada Pie

8 (6-inch) corn tortillas

1 jar (12 ounces) salsa

1 can (15½ ounces) kidney beans, drained and rinsed

1 cup shredded cooked chicken

1 cup (4 ounces) shredded Monterey Jack cheese with jalapeño peppers

Fresh cilantro and sliced red pepper (optional)

1. Prepare foil handles;* place in **CROCK-POT®** slow cooker. Place 1 tortilla on top of foil handles. Top with small amount of salsa, beans, chicken and cheese. Continue layering in order using remaining ingredients, ending with tortilla and cheese.

2. Cover; cook on LOW 6 to 8 hours or on HIGH 3 to 4 hours. Pull out by foil handles. Garnish with fresh cilantro and sliced red pepper, if desired.

Makes 4 to 6 servings

To make foil handles, tear off three (18×2-inch) strips of heavy foil or use regular foil folded to double thickness. Crisscross foil strips in spoke design and place in **CROCK-POT® slow cooker to make lifting tortilla stack easier.*

Hot & Sour Chicken

ETHNIC RECIPES

Manchego Eggplant

4 **large eggplants**

2 **tablespoons olive oil**

1 **cup flour**

1 **jar (25½ ounces) roasted garlic-flavor pasta sauce, divided**

2 **tablespoons Italian seasoning, divided**

1 **cup (4 ounces) grated manchego cheese, divided**

1 **jar (24 ounces) roasted eggplant flavor marinara, divided**

1. Peel eggplants and slice horizontally into ¾-inch-thick pieces. Place flour in shallow bowl. Dredge each slice of eggplant in flour to coat.

2. Heat oil in large skillet over medium-high heat. In batches, lightly brown eggplant on both sides.

3. Pour thin layer of roasted garlic-flavor pasta sauce into bottom of **CROCK-POT®** slow cooker. Top with, in order: eggplant slices, Italian seasoning, manchego cheese and roasted eggplant flavor marinara. Repeat layers until all ingredients have been used.

4. Cover and cook on HIGH 2 hours.

Makes 8 to 10 servings

SIDES IN A SNAP

Pesto Rice and Beans

1 can (15 ounces) Great Northern beans, rinsed and drained

1 can (14 ounces) chicken or vegetable broth

¾ cup uncooked long-grain white rice

1½ cups frozen cut green beans, thawed and drained

½ cup prepared pesto

Grated Parmesan cheese (optional)

1. Combine Great Northern beans, broth and rice in **CROCK-POT®** slow cooker. Cover; cook on LOW 2 hours.

2. Stir in green beans; cover and cook 1 hour more or until rice and beans are tender.

3. Turn off **CROCK-POT®** slow cooker and remove insert to heatproof surface. Stir in pesto and Parmesan cheese, if desired. Let stand, covered, 5 minutes or until cheese is melted. Serve immediately.

Makes 8 servings

Garden Potato Casserole

1¼ **pounds baking potatoes, unpeeled, sliced**

1 **small green or red bell pepper, thinly sliced**

¼ **cup finely chopped yellow onion**

2 **tablespoons butter, cut into pieces, divided**

½ **teaspoon salt**

½ **teaspoon dried thyme leaves**

Black pepper to taste

1 **small yellow squash, thinly sliced**

1 **cup (4 ounces) shredded sharp Cheddar cheese**

1. Place potatoes, bell pepper, onion, 1 tablespoon butter, salt, thyme and black pepper in **CROCK-POT®** slow cooker; mix well. Evenly layer squash over potato mixture; add remaining 1 tablespoon butter.

2. Cover; cook on LOW 7 hours or on HIGH 4 hours.

3. Remove potato mixture to serving bowl. Sprinkle with cheese; let stand 2 to 3 minutes or until cheese melts.

Makes 5 servings

Easy Dirty Rice

½ **pound bulk Italian sausage**

2 **cups water**

1 **cup uncooked long grain rice**

1 **large onion, finely chopped**

1 **large green bell pepper, finely chopped**

½ **cup finely chopped celery**

1½ **teaspoons salt**

½ **teaspoon ground red pepper**

½ **cup chopped fresh parsley (optional)**

1. Brown sausage in skillet 6 to 8 minutes over medium-high heat, stirring to break up meat. Drain fat. Place sausage in **CROCK-POT®** slow cooker.

2. Stir in all remaining ingredients except parsley. Cover; cook on LOW 2 hours. Stir in parsley, if desired.

Makes 4 servings

Barley with Currants and Pine Nuts

1 tablespoon unsalted butter

1 small onion, finely chopped

½ cup pearl barley

2 cups chicken or vegetable broth

½ teaspoon salt, or to taste

¼ teaspoon black pepper

⅓ cup currants

¼ cup pine nuts

1. Melt butter in small skillet over medium-high heat. Add onion. Cook and stir until lightly browned, about 2 minutes. Transfer to **CROCK-POT®** slow cooker. Add barley, broth, salt and pepper. Stir in currants. Cover; cook on LOW 3 hours.

2. Stir in pine nuts and serve immediately.

Makes 4 servings

Slow-Roasted Potatoes

16 small new potatoes

3 tablespoons butter, cut into small pieces

1 teaspoon paprika

½ teaspoon salt

¼ teaspoon garlic powder

Black pepper, to taste

Combine all ingredients in **CROCK-POT®** slow cooker; mix well. Cover; cook on LOW 7 hours or on HIGH 4 hours. Remove potatoes with slotted spoon to serving dish; cover with foil to keep warm. Add 1 to 2 tablespoons water to cooking liquid and stir until well blended. Pour over potatoes.

Makes 3 to 4 servings

Barley with Currants and Pine Nuts

Parmesan Potato Wedges

2 **pounds red potatoes, cut into ½-inch wedges**

¼ **cup finely chopped yellow onion**

1½ **teaspoons dried oregano**

½ **teaspoon salt**

Black pepper to taste

2 **tablespoons butter, cut into ⅛-inch pieces**

¼ **cup (1 ounce) grated Parmesan cheese**

Layer potatoes, onion, oregano, salt, pepper and butter in **CROCK-POT®** slow cooker. Cover; cook on HIGH 4 hours. Transfer potatoes to serving platter and sprinkle with cheese.

Makes 6 servings

102

Cheesy Corn and Peppers

2 pounds frozen corn kernels

2 tablespoons butter, cubed

2 poblano chile peppers, chopped *or* 1 large green bell pepper and 1 jalapeño pepper, seeded and finely chopped*

1 teaspoon salt

½ teaspoon ground cumin

¼ teaspoon black pepper

3 ounces cream cheese, cubed

1 cup (4 ounces) shredded sharp Cheddar cheese

Chile peppers can sting and irritate the skin; wear rubber gloves when handling peppers and do not touch eyes. Wash hands after handling.

Coat **CROCK-POT®** slow cooker with nonstick cooking spray. Add all ingredients except cream cheese and Cheddar cheese. Cover. Cook on HIGH 2 hours. Add cheeses; stir to blend. Cover. Cook 15 minutes more or until cheeses melt.

Makes 8 servings

SIDES IN A SNAP

Rustic Garlic Mashed Potatoes

2 pounds baking potatoes,
  unpeeled and cut into
  ½-inch cubes

¼ cup water

2 tablespoons butter,
  cut into ⅛-inch pieces

1¼ teaspoons salt

½ teaspoon garlic powder

¼ teaspoon black pepper

1 cup milk

Place all ingredients except milk in **CROCK-POT®** slow cooker; toss to combine. Cover; cook on LOW 7 hours or on HIGH 4 hours. Add milk to potatoes. Mash potatoes with potato masher or electric mixer until smooth.

Makes 5 servings

SIDES IN A SNAP

Chunky Ranch Potatoes

3 **pounds medium red potatoes, unpeeled and quartered**

1 **cup water**

½ **cup prepared ranch dressing**

½ **cup grated Parmesan or Cheddar cheese (optional)**

¼ **cup minced chives**

1. Place potatoes in **CROCK-POT®** slow cooker. Add water. Cover; cook on LOW 7 to 9 hours or on HIGH 4 to 6 hours or until potatoes are tender.

2. Stir in ranch dressing, cheese, if desired, and chives. Use spoon to break potatoes into chunks. Serve hot or cold.

Makes 8 servings

Gratin Potatoes with Asiago Cheese

6 **slices bacon, cut into 1-inch pieces**

6 **medium baking potatoes, peeled and thinly sliced**

½ **cup grated Asiago cheese**

Salt and black pepper, to taste

1½ **cups heavy cream**

1. Heat skillet over medium heat until hot. Add bacon. Cook and stir until crispy. Transfer to paper towel-lined plate with slotted spoon to drain.

2. Pour bacon fat from skillet into **CROCK-POT®** slow cooker. Layer one fourth of potatoes on bottom of **CROCK-POT®** slow cooker. Sprinkle one fourth of bacon over potatoes and top with one fourth of cheese. Add salt and pepper. Repeat layers. Pour cream over all. Cover; cook on LOW 7 to 9 hours or on HIGH 5 to 6 hours. Adjust salt and pepper, if desired.

Makes 4 to 6 servings

108

Chunky Ranch Potatoes

Spinach Gorgonzola Cornbread

2 boxes (8½ ounces each) cornbread mix

3 eggs

½ cup cream

1 box (10 ounces) frozen chopped spinach, thawed and drained

1 cup Gorgonzola crumbles

1 teaspoon black pepper

Paprika (optional)

Mix all ingredients except paprika in medium bowl. Spray inside of **CROCK-POT®** slow cooker with nonstick cooking spray. Pour batter into **CROCK-POT®** slow cooker; cover and cook 1½ hours on HIGH. Sprinkle top with paprika for more colorful crust, if desired.

Makes 10 to 12 servings

Note: *Cook only on HIGH setting for proper crust and texture.*

SIDES IN A SNAP

Sweet-Spiced Sweet Potatoes

2 **pounds sweet potatoes, peeled and cut into ½-inch pieces**

¼ **cup packed dark brown sugar**

1 **teaspoon ground cinnamon**

½ **teaspoon ground nutmeg**

⅛ **teaspoon salt**

2 **tablespoons butter, cut into ⅛-inch pieces**

1 **teaspoon vanilla**

Combine sweet potatoes, brown sugar, cinnamon, nutmeg and salt in **CROCK-POT®** slow cooker; mix well. Cover; cook on LOW 7 hours or on HIGH 4 hours. Add butter and vanilla; gently stir to blend.

Makes 4 servings

Orange-Spice Glazed Carrots

1 **package (32 ounces) baby carrots**

½ **cup packed light brown sugar**

½ **cup orange juice**

3 **tablespoons butter or margarine**

¾ **teaspoon ground cinnamon**

¼ **teaspoon ground nutmeg**

¼ **cup cold water**

2 **tablespoons cornstarch**

1. Combine carrots, brown sugar, orange juice, butter, cinnamon and nutmeg in **CROCK-POT®** slow cooker. Cover; cook on LOW 3½ to 4 hours or until carrots are crisp-tender.

2. Spoon carrots into serving bowl. Transfer juices to small saucepan. Bring to a boil.

3. Mix water and cornstarch in cup or small bowl until smooth; stir into saucepan. Boil 1 minute or until thickened, stirring constantly. Spoon over carrots.

Makes 6 servings

Swiss Cheese Scalloped Potatoes

2 pounds baking potatoes, peeled and thinly sliced, divided

½ cup finely chopped yellow onion, divided

¼ teaspoon salt, divided

¼ teaspoon ground nutmeg, divided

2 tablespoons butter, cut into small pieces, divided

½ cup milk

2 tablespoons all-purpose flour

3 ounces Swiss cheese slices, torn into small pieces

¼ cup finely chopped green onions (optional)

1. Layer half the potatoes, ¼ cup onion, ⅛ teaspoon salt, ⅛ teaspoon nutmeg and 1 tablespoon butter in **CROCK-POT®** slow cooker. Repeat layers. Cover; cook on LOW 7 hours or on HIGH 4 hours.

2. Remove potatoes with slotted spoon to serving dish and cover with foil to keep warm.

3. Blend milk and flour in small bowl until smooth. Stir mixture into cooking liquid. Add cheese; stir to combine. Turn **CROCK-POT®** slow cooker to HIGH. Cover; cook until slightly thickened, about 10 minutes. Stir. Pour cheese mixture over potatoes and serve. Garnish with chopped green onions, if desired.

Makes 5 to 6 servings

Tip: *Don't add water to the **CROCK-POT®** slow cooker, unless a recipe specifically says so. Foods don't lose much moisture during slow cooking, so follow recipe guidelines.*

PIECE OF CAKE

Cinn-Sational Swirl Cake

1 box (21½ ounces) cinnamon swirl cake mix

1 package (4-serving size) instant French vanilla pudding and pie filling mix

1 cup sour cream

1 cup cinnamon-flavored baking chips

1 cup water

¾ cup vegetable oil

Cinnamon ice cream (optional)

1. Coat 4½-quart **CROCK-POT®** slow cooker with nonstick cooking spray. Set cinnamon swirl mix packet aside. Mix remaining cake mix with French vanilla pudding and pie filling mix. Place in **CROCK-POT®** slow cooker.

2. Add sour cream, cinnamon chips, water and oil; stir well to combine. Batter will be slightly lumpy. Add reserved cinnamon swirl mix, slowly swirling through batter with knife. Cover; cook on LOW 3 to 4 hours or on HIGH 1½ to 1¾ hours or until toothpick inserted into center of cake comes out clean.

3. Serve warm with cinnamon ice cream, if desired.

Makes 10 to 12 servings

PIECE OF CAKE

Triple Chocolate Fantasy

2 pounds white almond bark, broken into pieces

1 bar (4 ounces) sweetened German chocolate, broken into pieces

1 package (12 ounces) semisweet chocolate chips

3 cups lightly toasted, coarsely chopped pecans

1. Place bark, German chocolate and chocolate chips in 3½- to 6-quart **CROCK-POT®** slow cooker. Cover; cook on HIGH 1 hour. Do not stir.

2. Turn **CROCK-POT®** slow cooker to LOW. Continue cooking 1 hour, stirring every 15 minutes. Stir in nuts.

3. Drop mixture by tablespoonfuls onto baking sheet covered with waxed paper; let cool. Store in tightly covered container.

Makes 36 pieces

Variation: *Instead of pecans, add raisins, crushed peppermint candy, candy-coated baking bits, crushed toffee, peanuts or pistachios, chopped gum drops, chopped dried fruit, candied cherries, chopped marshmallows or sweetened coconut.*

PIECE OF CAKE

Cherry Delight

1 can (21 ounces) cherry pie filling

1 package (18¼ ounces) yellow cake mix

½ cup (1 stick) butter, melted

⅓ cup chopped walnuts

Whipped topping or vanilla ice cream (optional)

Place pie filling in 2- to 4-quart **CROCK-POT®** slow cooker. Mix together cake mix and butter in medium bowl. Spread evenly over cherry filling. Sprinkle walnuts on top. Cover; cook on LOW 3 to 4 hours or on HIGH 1½ to 2 hours. Spoon into serving dishes and serve warm with whipped topping or ice cream, if desired.

Makes 8 to 10 servings

Pumpkin-Cranberry Custard

1 can (30 ounces) pumpkin pie filling

1 can (12 ounces) evaporated milk

1 cup dried cranberries

4 eggs, beaten

1 cup crushed or whole gingersnap cookies (optional)

Whipped cream (optional)

Combine pumpkin pie filling, evaporated milk, cranberries and eggs in 2½- to 4-quart **CROCK-POT®** slow cooker; mix thoroughly. Cover and cook on HIGH 4 to 4½ hours. Serve with crushed or whole gingersnaps and whipped cream, if desired.

Make 4 to 6 servings

Cherry Delight

PIECE OF CAKE

Easy Chocolate Pudding Cake

1 package (6-serving size) instant chocolate pudding and pie filling mix

3 cups milk

1 package (18¼ ounces) chocolate fudge cake mix plus ingredients to prepare mix

Whipped topping or ice cream (optional)

Crushed peppermint candies (optional)

1. Spray 4-quart **CROCK-POT®** slow cooker with nonstick cooking spray. Place pudding mix in **CROCK-POT®** slow cooker. Whisk in milk.

2. Prepare cake mix according to package directions. Carefully pour cake mix into **CROCK-POT®** slow cooker. **Do not stir.** Cover; cook on HIGH 1½ hours or until cake is set. Serve warm with whipped topping or ice cream and crushed peppermint candies, if desired.

Makes about 16 servings

PIECE OF CAKE

Streusel Pound Cake

1 **package (16 ounces) pound cake mix, plus ingredients to prepare mix**

¼ **cup packed light brown sugar**

1 **tablespoon all-purpose flour**

¼ **cup chopped nuts**

1 **teaspoon ground cinnamon**

Strawberries, blueberries, raspberries and/or powdered sugar (optional)

Coat inside of 1- to 1½-quart **CROCK-POT®** slow cooker with nonstick cooking spray. Prepare cake mix according to package directions; stir in brown sugar, flour, nuts and cinnamon. Pour batter into **CROCK-POT®** slow cooker. Cover; cook on HIGH 1½ to 1¾ hours or until toothpick inserted into center of cake comes out clean. Serve with berries and powdered sugar, if desired.

Makes 6 to 8 servings

PIECE OF CAKE

Cinnamon-Ginger Poached Pears

3 cups water

1 cup sugar

10 slices fresh ginger

2 whole cinnamon sticks

1 tablespoon candied ginger (optional)

6 Bosc or Anjou pears, peeled and cored

1. Combine water, sugar, ginger, cinnamon and candied ginger, if desired, in **CROCK-POT®** slow cooker. Add pears. Cover; cook on LOW 4 to 6 hours or on HIGH 1½ to 2 hours.

2. Remove pears. Cook syrup, uncovered, 30 minutes or until thickened.

Makes 6 servings

"Peachy Keen" Dessert Treat

1⅓ cups uncooked old-fashioned oats

1 cup granulated sugar

1 cup packed light brown sugar

⅔ cup buttermilk baking mix

2 teaspoons ground cinnamon

½ teaspoon ground nutmeg

2 pounds fresh peaches (about 8 medium), sliced

Combine oats, granulated sugar, brown sugar, baking mix, cinnamon and nutmeg in large bowl. Stir in peaches; mix until well blended. Pour mixture into 2½- to 4-quart **CROCK-POT®** slow cooker. Cover and cook on LOW 4 to 6 hours.

Makes 8 to 12 servings

126

Cinnamon-Ginger Poached Pears

PIECE OF CAKE

Citrus Chinese Dates with Toasted Hazelnuts

2 cups pitted dates

⅔ cup boiling water

½ cup sugar

Strips of peel from 1 lemon (yellow part only)

Whipped cream (optional)

¼ cup hazelnuts, shelled and toasted

1. Place dates in medium bowl and cover with water. Soak overnight to rehydrate. Drain and transfer dates to **CROCK-POT®** slow cooker.

2. Add ⅔ cup boiling water, sugar and lemon peel. Cover; cook on HIGH 3 hours.

3. Remove peel and discard. Place dates in serving dishes. Top with whipped cream, if desired, and sprinkle with toasted hazelnuts.

Makes 4 servings

Cherry Rice Pudding

1½ cups milk

1 cup hot cooked rice

3 eggs, beaten

½ cup sugar

¼ cup dried cherries or cranberries

½ teaspoon almond extract

¼ teaspoon salt

1. Combine all ingredients in large bowl. Pour mixture into greased 1½-quart casserole. Cover with foil.

2. Place rack in bottom of 5- to 6-quart **CROCK-POT®** slow cooker and pour in 1 cup water. Place casserole on rack. Cover; cook on LOW 4 to 5 hours.

3. Remove casserole from **CROCK-POT®** slow cooker. Let stand 15 minutes before serving.

Makes 6 servings

Citrus Chinese Dates with Toasted Hazelnuts

PIECE OF CAKE

Fresh Bosc Pear Granita

1 **pound fresh Bosc pears,
   cored, peeled and cubed**

1¼ **cups water**

¼ **cup sugar**

½ **teaspoon ground
   cinnamon**

1 **tablespoon lemon juice**

1. Place pears, water, sugar, and cinnamon in **CROCK-POT®** slow cooker. Cover; cook on HIGH 2½ to 3½ hours, or until pears are very soft and tender. Stir in lemon juice.

2. Transfer pears and syrup to blender or food processor and process mixture until smooth. Strain mixture through sieve. Discard any pulp. Pour liquid into 11×9-inch baking pan. Cover tightly with plastic wrap. Place pan in freezer.

3. Stir every hour while freezing, tossing granita with fork. Crush any lumps in mixture as it freezes. Freeze 3 to 4 hours, or until firm. You may keep granita in freezer up to 2 days before serving; toss granita every 6 to 12 hours.

Makes 6 servings

PIECE OF CAKE

Spicy Fruit Dessert

¼ cup orange marmalade

¼ teaspoon pumpkin pie spice

1 can (6 ounces) frozen orange juice concentrate

2 cups canned pears, drained and diced

2 cups carambola (star fruit), sliced and seeds removed

1. Combine marmalade, pumpkin pie spice, orange juice concentrate, pears and carambola in **CROCK-POT®** slow cooker.

2. Cover; cook on LOW 4 to 6 hours or on HIGH 2 to 3 hours or until done. Serve warm over pound cake or ice cream.

Makes 4 to 6 servings

Poached Pears with Raspberry Sauce

4 cups cran-raspberry juice
cocktail

2 cups Rhine or Riesling
wine

¼ cup sugar

2 cinnamon sticks, broken
into halves

4 to 5 firm Bosc or Anjou
pears, peeled

1 package (10 ounces)
frozen raspberries in
syrup, thawed

Fresh berries (optional)

1. Combine juice, wine, sugar and cinnamon stick halves in **CROCK-POT®** slow cooker. Submerge pears in mixture. Cover; cook on LOW 3½ to 4 hours or until pears are tender.

2. Remove and discard cinnamon sticks.

3. Process raspberries in food processor or blender until smooth; strain and discard seeds. Spoon raspberry sauce onto serving plates; place pears on top of sauce. Garnish with fresh berries.

Makes 4 to 5 servings

Chocolate Croissant Pudding

1½ **cups milk**

3 **eggs**

½ **cup sugar**

¼ **cup unsweetened cocoa powder**

½ **teaspoon vanilla**

¼ **teaspoon salt**

2 **plain croissants, cut into 1-inch pieces, divided**

½ **cup chocolate chips, divided**

Whipped cream

1. Coat 1-quart casserole, soufflé dish or other high-sided baking pan with nonstick cooking spray.

2. Beat milk, eggs, sugar, cocoa, vanilla and salt in medium bowl. Layer half of croissants, ¼ cup chocolate chips and half of egg mixture into prepared casserole. Repeat layers with remaining croissants, chocolate chips and egg mixture.

3. Place rack or trivet in **CROCK-POT®** slow cooker; pour in 1 cup water. Place filled casserole on rack. Cover; cook on LOW 3 to 4 hours.

4. Remove casserole from **CROCK-POT®** slow cooker. Spoon bread pudding into bowls. Top with whipped cream.

Makes 6 servings

Tip: *Straight-sided round casserole or soufflé dishes that fit into the* **CROCK-POT®** *stoneware make excellent baking dishes for breads, cakes, and desserts.*

INDEX

INDEX

INDEX

INDEX

INDEX

INDEX

METRIC CHART

VOLUME MEASUREMENTS (dry)

⅛ teaspoon = 0.5 mL
¼ teaspoon = 1 mL
½ teaspoon = 2 mL
¾ teaspoon = 4 mL
1 teaspoon = 5 mL
1 tablespoon = 15 mL
2 tablespoons = 30 mL
¼ cup = 60 mL
⅓ cup = 75 mL
½ cup = 125 mL
⅔ cup = 150 mL
¾ cup = 175 mL
1 cup = 250 mL
2 cups = 1 pint = 500 mL
3 cups = 750 mL
4 cups = 1 quart = 1 L

VOLUME MEASUREMENTS (fluid)

1 fluid ounce (2 tablespoons) = 30 mL
4 fluid ounces (½ cup) = 125 mL
8 fluid ounces (1 cup) = 250 mL
12 fluid ounces (1½ cups) = 375 mL
16 fluid ounces (2 cups) = 500 mL

WEIGHTS (mass)

½ ounce = 15 g
1 ounce = 30 g
3 ounces = 90 g
4 ounces = 120 g
8 ounces = 225 g
10 ounces = 285 g
12 ounces = 360 g
16 ounces = 1 pound = 450 g

DIMENSIONS

1/16 inch = 2 mm
⅛ inch = 3 mm
¼ inch = 6 mm
½ inch = 1.5 cm
¾ inch = 2 cm
1 inch = 2.5 cm

OVEN TEMPERATURES

250°F = 120°C
275°F = 140°C
300°F = 150°C
325°F = 160°C
350°F = 180°C
375°F = 190°C
400°F = 200°C
425°F = 220°C
450°F = 230°C

BAKING PAN AND DISH EQUIVALENTS

Utensil	Size in Inches	Size in Centimeters	Volume	Metric Volume
Baking or Cake Pan (square or rectangular)	8×8×2	20×20×5	8 cups	2 L
	9×9×2	23×23×5	10 cups	2.5 L
	13×9×2	33×23×5	12 cups	3 L
Loaf Pan	8½×4½×2½	21×11×6	6 cups	1.5 L
	9×9×3	23×13×7	8 cups	2 L
Round Layer Cake Pan	8×1½	20×4	4 cups	1 L
	9×1½	23×4	5 cups	1.25 L
Pie Plate	8×1½	20×4	4 cups	1 L
	9×1½	23×4	5 cups	1.25 L
Baking Dish or Casserole			1 quart/4 cups	1 L
			1½ quart/6 cups	1.5 L
			2 quart/8 cups	2 L
			3 quart/12 cups	3 L

144